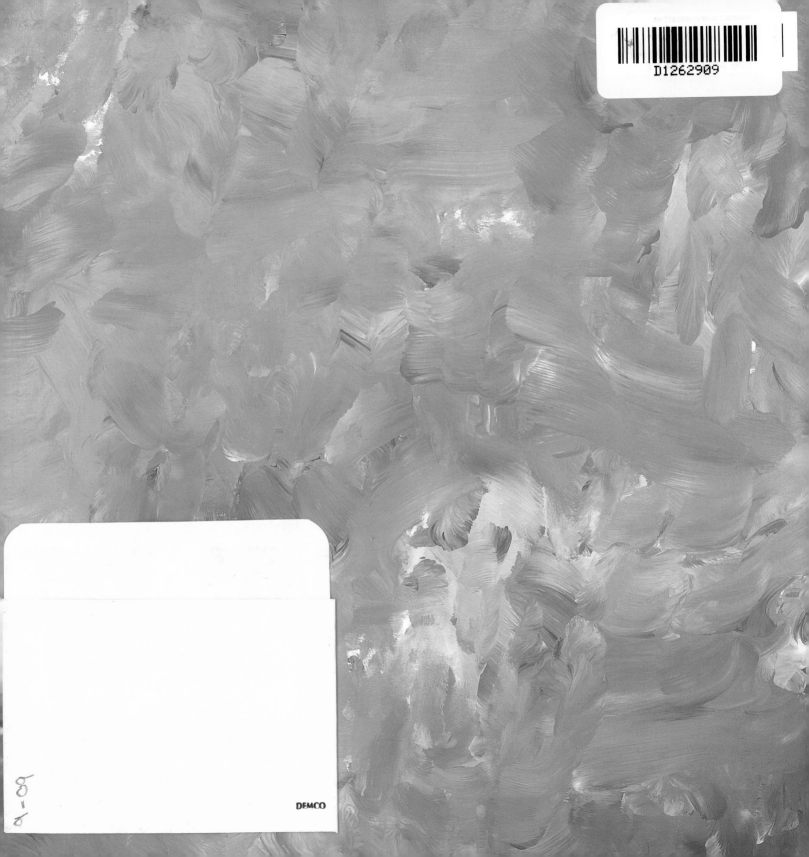

Copyright © 2008 by Lisa Campbell Ernst • Printed in China • All rights reserved CIP Data is available. • ISBN: 978-1-934706-01-5 • Blue Apple Books • 515 Valley Street, Maplewood, NJ 07040 • www.blueapplebooks.com • Distributed in the U.S. by Chronicle Books

3 5 7 9 10 8 6 4 2

**For Elizabeth
and Allison
—L. C. E.**

Lisa Campbell Ernst

Round Like a Ball!

Blue Apple Books

Let's play a guessing game.

I'm thinking
of something
that is . . .

round like a ball.

?

"I love balls!"
barked the dog.

Wait! Here's another clue.

It's round like a ball

and is quite beautiful.

"Is it a fancy pearl?"
asked the sister.

Good guess.
But it's not
a pearl.

It's round like a ball and has many, many colors.

"I know, it's a gumball machine!" guessed the brother.

No.
It's not
a gumball
machine.

It's round like a ball

and is always moving.

No, it's not a ball
for juggling.

It's round like a ball,

and it nourishes us.

"Maybe it's a ball for juggling,"
guessed the mom.

"Is it a berry?"
asked the dad.

No, it's not a berry.
Here's another clue.

It's round like a ball

and is hot and cold.

Good guesses.
But it's not
ice cream or a
matzoh ball.

It's round like a ball

and is wet and dry.

"A fishbowl!" meowed the cat.

No, it's not
a fishbowl.
Here's another
clue.

It's round like a ball

and is surrounded by air.

"Is it a balloon?"
asked the grandpa.

No, it's not
a balloon.

It's round like a ball

and is hard and strong.

"I think it's a rock,"
said the aunt.

No, it's not
a rock.

It's round like a ball and must be handled with care.

"It could be a bubble,"
said the uncle.

It's not a bubble.
Here's the
last clue:

It's round like a ball

and home to us all.

What do you

think it is?

It's the Earth!

Everyone celebrated!

The Earth
is beautiful
and always moving.

The Earth
is every color of
the rainbow.

The Earth
is round
like a ball.

The Earth
is both hot and cold,
and wet and dry.

The Earth
nourishes us all. It's hard
and strong, but it's also
fragile and needs
to be handled
with care.

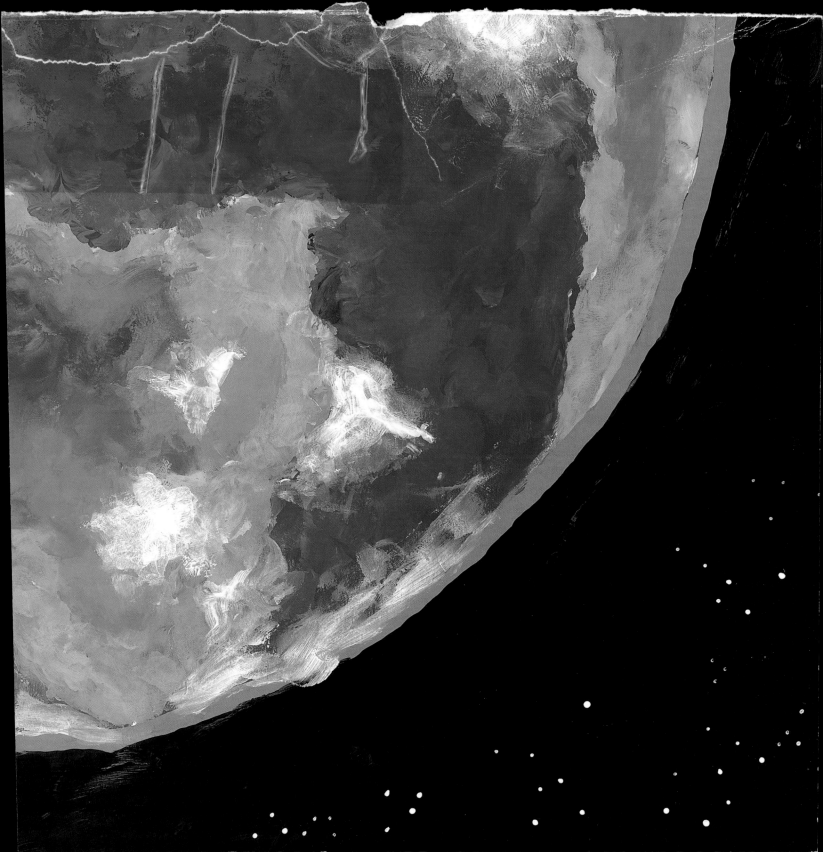

You can help take care of the Earth. Here are some ways:

- Recycle plastic, glass, metal, cardboard, and paper.

- Plant flowers in your garden that will attract butterflies and bees.

- Use refillable water bottles and avoid bottled water.

- Turn off the water while brushing your teeth.

- Give away outgrown clothes or toys so they can be recycled.

- Turn off the lights and television when you leave a room.

- Pick up litter in your neighborhood.

- Watch less TV and play fewer electronic games.